Dec 27, 2004

Happy B

From your friend,

melody

Remember When...?

Remember Thelonius Monk and Mitch Miller?
How about paint-by-number kits, or hula hoops?
Can you remember when cramming a phone booth was common,
or when Elvis Presley was uncommonly cool?
When "way, way out" was just about as "in" as you could get?

Then you must be ready for a 50s party!

THIS BOOK OF MEMORIES PRESENTED TO:

_____

ON THE OCCASION OF:

_____

DATE:

SETTING THE SCENE

1952
- Puerto Rico becomes an independent commonwealth of the US
- British Overseas Airways inaugurates the world's first commercial jet passenger service
- George Jorgenson has the first sex change operation in medical history, in Copenhagen

1953
- Joseph Stalin dies of mysterious causes
- Dwight D. Eisenhower is inaugurated as the 34th president of the United States
- Elizabeth II is crowned Queen of England

1950
- The Peanuts comic strip is born, debuting in seven newspapers
- Ralphe Bunche becomes the first black to win the Nobel peace prize for negotiating an end to the Arab-Israeli war of 1948
- The Brink's armored car depot in Boston is robbed of $2.7 million
- The FBI issues its first list of the Ten Most Wanted Criminals
- Smokey the Bear becomes the living symbol of the US Forestry Service

1954
- The US Navy launches Nautilus, its first nuclear-powered submarine
- Joe DiMaggio and Marilyn Monroe marry; nine months later she files for divorce
- J.R.R. Tolkien's *The Lord of The Rings* is published
- The Miss America Pageant is televised for the first time

1956
- James Dean dies in a car crash in California
- Ray Kroc opens the first McDonald's in Des Plaines, Illinois
- Walt Disney Incorporated opens Disneyland in Anaheim, California
- The Ann Landers advice column is launched in the *Chicago Sun Times*

1951
- The 22nd Amendment to the constitution is adopted, limiting the presidency to two terms
- UNIVAC, the first general-purpose electronic computer, is dedicated at the Census Bureau in Philadelphia

1955
- Elvis Presley appears on the Ed Sullivan show, but only from the waist up
- Movie star Grace Kelly weds Prince Rainier III of Monaco
- Italian ocean liner Andrea Doria sinks off Nantucket after colliding with the Swedish liner Stockholm

1957
- Collier's magazine issues its final edition
- The Baby Boom peaks with a record 4.3 million babies born in the US

1958
- The hula hoop craze takes off
- The cost of a stamp rises a penny, from 3¢; the first increase in 26 years
- NASA is established
- Van Cliburn is the first American to win the International Tchaikovsky Piano Competition in Moscow

1959
- Manhattan's Guggenheim Museum opens
- Buddy Holly, Ritchie Valens and The Big Bopper die in a plane crash while on tour
- Louis Leakey discovers 1.75 million-year-old skull fragments in the Olduvai Gorge
- Mattel introduces the Barbie doll

THE BUZZ

- Grandma Moses
- Modern Art
- Horror Comics
- Playboy Foldouts
- MAD Magazine
- TV Guide
- Non Violence / Civil Disobedience
- Zen
- Blacklist
- Marilyn Monroe
- Flying Saucers
- Beatniks / Beat Generation / Bohemians
- Segregation

TOP OF THE CHARTS

- **COME ON-A MY HOUSE** • *Rosemary Clooney*
- **MR. SANDMAN** • *The Chordettes*
- **O MY PAPA** • *Eddie Fisher*
- **TENNESSEE WALTZ** • *Patti Page*
- **FEVER** • *Peggy Lee*
- **MACK THE KNIFE** • *Bobby Darin*
- **POOR LITTLE FOOL** • *Ricky Nelson*
- **ALL I HAVE TO DO IS DREAM** • *The Everly Brothers*
- **BLUE SUEDE SHOES** • *Elvis Presley*
- **HEARTBRAKE HOTEL** • *Elvis Presley*
- **DON'T BE CRUEL** • *Elvis Presley*
- **LOVE ME TENDER** • *Elvis Presley*
- **ROCK AROUND THE CLOCK** • *Bill Haley and the Comets*
- **THREE COINS IN THE FOUNTAIN** • *The Four Aces*
- **MELODY OF LOVE** • *Billy Vaughn*
- **YELLOW ROSE OF TEXAS** • *Mitch Miller*
- **UNCHAINED MELODY** • *Les Baxter*
- **GREAT PRETENDER** • *The Platters*
- **WHATEVER WILL BE, WILL BE** • *Doris Day*
- **THEME FROM "PICNIC"** • *Morris Stoloff*
- **TAMMY** • *Debbie Reynolds*
- **LOVE LETTERS IN THE SAND** • *Pat Boone*
- **CHANCES ARE** • *Johnny Mathis*
- **BYE BYE LOVE** • *The Everly Brothers*
- **YOUNG LOVE** • *Tab Hunter*
- **VOLARE** • *Domenico Modugno*
- **TEQUILA** • *The Champs*
- **BATTLE OF NEW ORLEANS** • *Johnny Horton*
- **LONELY BOY** • *Paul Anka*
- **THIRD MAN THEME** • *Anton Karas*
- **MONA LISA** • *Nat "King" Cole*
- **HOW HIGH THE MOON** • *Les Paul and Mary Ford*
- **YOUNG AT HEART** • *Frank Sinatra*
- **CRY** • *Johnnie Ray*

THE BUZZ

Axe
Lena Horne
Chuck Berry's Duck Walk
Peggy Lee
Jazz
Miles Davis
Rock and Roll
Conga Drums
Payola Scandal
Jerry Lee Lewis
Frank Sinatra
Mario Lanza
Dinah Shore
Tony Bennett

CARE TO DANCE?

THE MAMBO
The Bunny Hop   The Hand Jive
CHA CHA
Bossa Nova
THE STROLL
The Chicken, the Greasy Chicken
THE BOP
Rock and Stomp

We Loved Our Television

- WAGON TRAIN
- MAVERICK
- I LOVE LUCY
- ED SULLIVAN SHOW
- MY LITTLE MARGIE
- NAME THAT TUNE
- WHAT'S MY LINE?
- GUNSMOKE
- HAVE GUN, WILL TRAVEL
- KUKLA, FRAN, AND OLLIE
- THE LONE RANGER
- HOPALONG CASSIDY
- THE HONEYMOONERS
- THE ADVENTURES OF OZZIE & HARRIET
- DAVY CROCKETT ON DISNEYLAND TV SHOW
- AMERICAN BANDSTAND [DICK CLARK]
- DOBIE GILLIS
- FATHER KNOWS BEST
- LEAVE IT TO BEAVER
- OUR MISS BROOKS
- THE JACK BENNY SHOW
- MR. PEEPERS
- ALFRED HITCHCOCK PRESENTS
- THE LAWRENCE WELK SHOW
- MAKE ROOM FOR DADDY
- CHEYENNE
- DRAGNET
- MICKEY MOUSE CLUB
- NAKED CITY
- CAPTAIN KANGAROO
- YOU ARE THERE
- HALL OF FAME THEATRE
- MEET THE PRESS
- TOAST OF THE TOWN
- PETER GUNN
- 77 SUNSET STRIP
- PERRY MASON
- YOUR SHOW OF SHOWS
- THE ADVENTURES OF RIN-TIN-TIN

THE BUZZ

- Fess Parker
- Coonskin caps
- Burns & Allen
- Mort Sahl
- Lip synching
- Roy Rogers and Dale Evans
- "Only the names were changed to protect the innocent"
- Justine Corelli, Kenny Rossi
- Desi Arnaz

SLANG OF THE 50s

- Egghead
- Hairy
- Hang Loose
- cool, hip, smooth, neat
- real George
- Wheels
- Cat
- Passion Pit
- Flip
- with it
- square, yo-yo, nerd, L7, cube
- DDT (drop dead twice)
- Tough
- Pad
- Blast off (get lost)
- Dig it
- Bread, green
- rock-bottom
- Grounded
- Chick

MOVIES WE HAD TO SEE:

* BORN YESTERDAY
* CYRANO DE BERGERAC
* GIDGET
* A SUMMER PLACE
* THE AFRICAN QUEEN
* A STREETCAR NAMED DESIRE
* DIAL M FOR MURDER
* REAR WINDOW
* TO CATCH A THIEF
* EAST OF EDEN
* GIANT
* REBEL WITHOUT A CAUSE
* ROOM AT THE TOP
* HIGH NOON
* COME BACK, LITTLE SHEBA
* STALAG 17
* ROMAN HOLIDAY
* THE COUNTRY GIRL
* THE KING AND I
* ANASTASIA
* THE THREE FACES OF EVE
* SEPARATE TABLES
* I WANT TO LIVE!

Academy Award® Best Pictures

1950 ....All About Eve
1951 ....An American in Paris
1952 ......The Greatest Show on Earth
1953 ....From Here to Eternity
1954 ....On the Waterfront
1955 ....Marty
1956 ....Around the World in 80 Days
1957 ....The Bridge on the River Kwai
1958 ....Gigi
1959 ....Ben-Hur

PERSONALITIES

THE BIG KAHUNA
YUL BRYNNER
GRACE KELLY
DAVID NIVEN
SUSAN HAYWARD
MARILYN MONROE
ALEC GUINNESS
JOANNE WOODWARD
MARTIN & LEWIS
MARLON BRANDO

HUMPHREY BOGART
ERNEST BORGNINE
AUDREY HEPBURN
WILLIAM HOLDEN
GARY COOPER
SHIRLEY BOOTH
VIVIEN LEIGH
JOSE FERRER
JUDY HOLLIDAY
CHARLTON HESTON

On Broadway

- THE MUSIC MAN
- MY FAIR LADY
- THE KING AND I
- FLOWER DRUM SONG
- THE SOUND OF MUSIC
- BYE, BYE, BIRDIE
- WEST SIDE STORY
- THE THREE-PENNY OPERA
- GUYS AND DOLLS
- THE PAJAMA GAME
- GYPSY

LIFE MAGAZINE

*

The Caine Mutiny
HERMAN WOUK

*

The Catcher in the Rye
J. D. SALINGER

*

Invisible Man
RALPH ELLISON

*

Peyton Place
GRACE METALIOUS

The Old Man and the Sea
ERNEST HEMINGWAY

*

On the Road
JACK KEROUAC

*

The Cardinal
HENRY MORTON ROBINSON

*

From Here to Eternity
JAMES JONES

*

Exodus
LEON URIS

*

Doctor Zhivago
BORIS PASTERNAK

Gift From the Sea
ANNE MORROW LINDBERGH

*

Notes of a Native Son
JAMES BALDWIN

*

Please Don't Eat the Daisies
JEAN KERR

*

Kon-Tiki
THOR HEYERDAHL

*

The Power of Positive Thinking
NORMAN VINCENT PEALE

*

The Status Seekers
VANCE PACKARD

On The Bookshelf

Sexual Behavior in the Human Female
ALFRED KINSEY

A Stillness at Appomattox
BRUCE CATTON

The Man in the Gray Flannel Suit
SLOAN WILSON

The Cat in the Hat
DR. SEUSS

Breakfast at Tiffany's
TRUMAN CAPOTE

The Search for Bridey Murphy
MOREY BERNSTEIN

'Twixt Twelve and Twenty
PAT BOONE

Hawaii
JAMES MICHENER

Goodbye, Columbus
PHILIP ROTH

WHERE WERE YOU

1950
- North Korean troops invade South Korea; the US and UN rally to its support
- Alger Hiss, under investigation for Communist ties, is convicted of perjury
- Televised hearings on organized crime, chaired by Senator Estes Kefauver, begin
- Truman orders the development of the hydrogen bomb
- The House Un-American Activities Committee begins its dirty work

1951
- General Douglas MacArthur is relieved of his command in Asia by President Truman

1952
- Republican and Democratic national conventions are covered on TV, and the nation is transfixed
- Richard Nixon gives the Checkers speech, to deny using his secret slush fund for personal expenses
- The US explodes the first hydrogen bomb in the Marshall Islands

1953
- Earl Warren, governor of California, is appointed Chief Justice of the Supreme Court by President Eisenhower
- Julius and Ethel Rosenberg are executed for espionage
- The armistice ending the Korean War is signed at Panmunjom

1954
- The US armed forces are desegregated, with the abolition of all-Negro units
- Communists force the French out of Vietnam, its colony for 87 years
- In Brown vs. Board of Education of Topeka, Kansas, the Supreme Court unanimously bans racial segregation in public schools
- Legislation adds the words "under God" to the Pledge of Allegiance

1955
- Rosa Parks refuses to give up her seat on the bus in Montgomery, Alabama, to a white man, inaugurating the civil rights movement
- The AFL and the CIO labor unions merge
- West Germany becomes a sovereign state
- The Warsaw Pact, an east European mutual defense agreement, is signed

WHEN...

1956
- After a year-long boycott of public transportation in Montgomery, Alabama, the US Supreme Court declares bus segregation illegal
- "In God We Trust" becomes the motto of the US and is added to coins and currency
- Eisenhower is elected for a second term
- The Federal Aid Highway Act authorizes 41,000 miles of interstate roads

1957
- Eisenhower sends federal troops to Little Rock, Arkansas, to protect nine black students as they attend the all-white Central High School
- The Soviets launch Sputinik I, the first man-made satellite, into orbit
- Congress establishes the Civil Rights Commission

1958
- The US launches its first satellite, Explorer I
- Nikita Khrushchev assumes leadership of the Communist party and the government of the Soviet Union
- The FAA is established to control civilian and military air traffic
- A scandal in TV quiz shows is revealed when Twenty One and its contestant Charles Van Doren are exposed as frauds

1959
- Richard Nixon and Nikita Khrushchev have their friendly "kitchen debate"
- Fidel Castro's guerilla forces overthrow Cuban dictator Fulgencio Batista
- Alaska and Hawaii become the 49th and 50th states

THE BUZZ

- I Like Ike
- 38th Parallel
- Adlai Stevenson
- Fallout Shelter
- Martin Luther King Jr.
- Duck and Cover
- Police Action
- Red Scare
- McCarthyism

WHAT WE WORE

- DUCKTAIL HAIRCUT
- THE POODLE CUT
- HEAD SCARVES
- BERET
- STARCHED PETTICOATS
- PULLOVER SWEATER WITH DETACHABLE COLLAR
- CHARM BRACELET
- INITIAL PIN
- SADDLE SHOES
- PONYTAIL
- FLATTOP HAIRCUT
- SWEATER SETS
- STRING OF PEARLS
- PENNY LOAFERS
- WHITE SOCKS
- CIRCLE SKIRT
- STRAPLESS DRESS
- SHORT SHORTS
- BERMUDA SHORTS
- LOUD SPORTS SHIRTS
- LETTER SWEATER
- PEGGED PANTS
- COLOR: PINK

THE BUZZ

- Greaser
- Hope Chest
- Neighborhood Cocktail Parties
- cramming (boys into phone booths for example)
- Baton-Twirling
- Joe College
- first supermodel: Suzy Parker
- The Prom
- Going Steady
- Tabu, Tigress, Evening in Paris
- Poodle Paraphernalia

If you had wheels, you had to drive a...

- HOT ROD
- BUICK SKYLARK CONVERTIBLE
- CADILLAC
- CORVETTE
- CHEVROLET BEL AIR
- FORD THUNDERBIRD
- DESOTO

Popular Vacation Destinations

- MAZATLAN, MEXICO
- CROSS-COUNTRY DRIVING VACATIONS
- CAMPING
- HAVANA, CUBA
- MUSCLE BEACH (SANTA MONICA, CA)
- KATHMANDU, NEPAL

LIFESTYLES — 1950s

California Dip

1 envelope dry Onion Soup mix
2 cups sour cream

Mix Onion Soup and sour cream and let stand for one hour. Serve with raw vegetables for dipping.

SPAM Bean Bake

1 whole SPAM Slice into 8 slices
1 large can baked beans
2 T. molasses
2 T. brown sugar
1 t. dry mustard

Combine baked beans, molasses, brown sugar and mustard. Place into greased casserole dish. Top with SPAM slices. Bake at 350° for 25 minutes. Serves 4.

WHO WON? THE WORLD SERIES

1950 ....New York Yankees 4, Philadelphia Phillies 0
1951 ....New York Yankees 4, New York Giants 2
1952............New York Yankees 4, Brooklyn Dodgers 3
1953.............New York Yankees 4, Brooklyn Dodgers 2
1954 ....New York Giants 4, Cleveland Indians 0
1955............Brooklyn Dodgers 4, New York Yankees 3
1956............New York Yankees 4, Brooklyn Dodgers 3
1957 ....Milwaukee Braves 4, New York Yankees 3
1958 ....New York Yankees 4, Milwaukee Braves 3
1959......Los Angeles Dodgers 4, Chicago White Sox 2

WHO WON? THE NFL CHAMPIONSHIP

1950.........Cleveland Browns 30, Los Angeles Rams 28
1951.........Los Angeles Rams 24, Cleveland Browns 17
1952....................Detroit Lions 17 Cleveland Browns 7
1953 ....Detroit Lions 17, Cleveland 16
1954..................Cleveland Browns 56, Detroit Lions 10
1955........Cleveland Browns 38, Los Angeles Rams 14
1956.................New York Giants 47, Chicago Bears 7
1957 ....Detroit Lions 59, Cleveland Browns 14
1958 ....Baltimore Colts 23, New York Giants 17
1959 ....Baltimore Colts 31, New York Giants 16

THE NBA CHAMPIONSHIP

1950
Minneapolis Lakers 4
Syracuse Nationals 2

1951
Rochester Royals 4
New York Knicks 3

1952
Minneapolis Lakers 4
New York Knicks 3

1953
Minneapolis Lakers 4
New York Knicks 1

1954
Minneapolis Lakers 4
Syracuse Nationals 3

1955
Syracuse Nationals 4
Fort Wayne Pistons 3

1956
Philadelphia Warriors 4
Fort Wayne Pistons 1

1957
Boston Celtics 4
St. Louis Hawks 3

1958
St. Louis Hawks 4
Boston Celtics 2

1959
Boston Celtics 4
Minneapolis Lakers 0

WHO WON? THE STANLEY CUP

1950 .... Detroit Red Wings 4, New York Rangers 3
1951 .... Toronto Maple Leafs 4, Montreal Canadiens 1
1952 .... Detroit Red Wings 4, Montreal Canadiens 0
1953 .... Montreal Canadiens 4, Boston Bruins 1
1954 .... Detroit Red Wings 4, Montreal Canadiens 3
1955 .... Detroit Red Wings 4, Montreal Canadiens 3
1956 .... Montreal Canadiens 4, Detroit Red Wings 1
1957 .... Montreal Canadiens 4, Boston Bruins 1
1958 .... Montreal Canadiens 4, Boston Bruins 2
1959 .... Montreal Canadiens 4, Toronto Maple Leafs 1

THE BUZZ

bowling
Golfing
Little League
Girls' sports
Rocky Marciano
Mickey Mantle
Wilt Chamberlain
Willie Mays
Bill Russell
Hank Aaron

A DECADE OF SPORTS

1950
- Babe Zaharias-Didrikson creates the Ladies Professional Golf Association
- Sugar Ray Robinson defeats Jake "Raging Bull" LaMotta for the middleweight championship of the world

1951
- Joe DiMaggio retires with a lifetime batting average of .325 and a total of 361 home runs
- Ted Williams (Boston Red Sox) becomes the highest-paid baseball player
- "The Giants win the pennant! The Giants win the pennant!"

1952
- Automatic pin spotters at the bowling alley spell the end of pin boys
- Winter Olympic Games are held in Oslo, Norway
- Summer Olympic Games are held in Helsinki, Finland
- Bob Mathias breaks his own decathlon record for an unprecedented second gold medal

1953
- Edmund Hillary and Tenzing Norgay reach the pinnacle of Mount Everest
- Ben Hogan is the first golfer to sweep the US Open, the Masters, and the British Open in a single year
- The NY Yankees become the first team in baseball history to win five consecutive World Series
- Maureen Connelly is the first woman to win the Grand Slam in tennis: the Australian, French, and US Open and Wimbledon women's singles titles

1954
- Roger Bannister breaks the 4-minute mile at a track and field meet in Oxford, England
- *Sports Illustrated* begins publication
- Arnold Palmer wins the US Amateur golf championship, his first major victory

1956
- Don Larsen throws a perfect game for the Yankees in the fifth game of the World Series
- Winter Olympics held in Cortina d'Ampezzo, Italy
- Summer Games held in Melbourne, Australia (except for the equestrian events, which were held in Stockholm, Sweden)
- Tenley Albright is the first American woman to win an Olympic gold medal in figure skating
- Floyd Patterson knocks out Archie Moore to become the youngest heavyweight champion in history at age 21

1957
- Althea Gibson becomes the first black athlete to win at Wimbledon

1958
- Baseball's New York Giants and Brooklyn Dodgers move to the West coast, settling in San Francisco and Los Angeles

LIFE JUST WOULDN'T BE THE SAME WITHOUT...

★ Miss Clairol hair coloring
★ Diners Club credit card
★ Xerox copy machine
★ Play-Doh modeling compound
★ Pampers disposable diapers
★ Con-Tact paper
★ Flouridation in public drinking water
★ Sony pocket-sized transistor radios
★ Metracal diet drink
★ Polio vaccine
★ Power steering by Chrysler Corp.
★ Kidney transplants
★ Color television

THE BUZZ

Suburbia
commuters
Free maps
pole lamps **Lincoln Logs**
Flamingos on the lawn
"Atom" clock **Silly Putty**
"See the USA in your Chevrolet"
buy now, pay later **backyard barbeque**
air raid shelters
babysitters (50¢/hour)
Vacation decals
S&H trading stamps
whitewall tires
Erector sets
den mothers
Portable record players
Mr. Potato Head

CHECKLIST FOR THE PERFECT PARTY

THREE WEEKS BEFORE:

- [ ] Plan the occasion *> a 50s nostalgia party*
- [ ] Create a compatible guest list
- [ ] Choose a location that will accommodate the number of guests
- [ ] Send invitations [date, time (start/end), place, directions] *> Ask guests to dress in clothing of the era*
- [ ] Plan and select decorations *> This can include old yearbooks, record albums and other memorabilia*
- [ ] Begin collecting materials and creating props
   > Visit garage sales for old 45s and LPs, even old clothes   > Movie memorabilia stores are good sources
- [ ] Prepare menu and grocery list *> Consider using food from the era for extra nostalgia*
- [ ] Select and hire caterer/serving help (if using)

A FEW DAYS BEFORE:

- [ ] Call any guests who have not responded
- [ ] Buy groceries and beverages
- [ ] Prepare and refrigerate/freeze food items that can be made in advance
- [ ] Make party costume or select outfit

ONE DAY BEFORE:

- [ ] Clean house, party room facility or other party site
- [ ] Set up and arrange party room
- [ ] Thaw out frozen party foods
- [ ] Get out serving pieces
- [ ] Coordinate last-minute arrangements with caterer, servers (if using)

THE DAY OF:

- [ ] Decorate party room
- [ ] Prepare and arrange remaining food
- [ ] Coordinate set-up, service, cleanup with hired helpers (if using)
- [ ] Mentally travel through party *> BEGINNING: arrivals and introductions   > MIDDLE: food and activities; have everyone sign the book   > END: wrap it up! Party favors, Polaroid photos*
- [ ] Dress in party outfit
- [ ] Await guests
- [ ] Have a good time!

HAPPY DAY!

Hope You Enjoyed Your Party... We Sure Did!

Celebrating You and the 1950s
©2004 Elm Hill Books
ISBN: 1404184740

In some cases, quoted material for this book was obtained from secondary sources, primarily print media. While every effort was made to ensure the accuracy of these sources, the accuracy cannot be guaranteed.

All rights reserved. Except for brief quotations used in reviews, articles or other media, no part of this book may be reproduced or transmitted in any form or by any means, electronic or mechanical, including photocopying, recording, or by information storage or retrieval system, without the express, written consent of the publisher.

For additions, deletions, corrections or clarifications in future editions of this text, please contact Paul Shepherd, Senior Acquisitions and Development Editor for Elm Hill Books.

Manuscript written and compiled by Jamie Chavez.

Layout and design created by Susan Rae Stegall of D/SR Design, LLC.

Front cover photo by Jackson DeParis Photography.

Music tracks courtesy of Everest Records.